RIRI'S ADVICE

TO THE GRANDS

FIRST EDITION

Interior Graphics and Cover Design by Marie W. Watts

Book Design and Typography by Gregory Walker

Cover Photography by Karen W. Lively

ISBN   979-8-218-27365-1

RIRI'S ADVICE

TO THE GRANDS

Marie W. Watts

LAS TORTUGAS
PRESS

RIRI'S ADVICE TO THE GRANDS

Dear Grands,

In seventy-two years, I've learned many lessons in living. It's not all been easy or fun, but I keep on keeping on. Each phase of my life brings new joy and wonder. I want the best for you and think sharing my discoveries may make your journey a bit easier.

Unfortunately, no road map exists that will make your life perfect, but I can supply tools. The more you have, the better you can navigate life's ups and downs. One screwdriver doesn't fit all screws, and one behavior doesn't fit all life situations. These tools are delicate and complex, not like a hammer. Practice and think about them constantly.

To me, life is a system like a big clock. The gears (pieces of our life) are interrelated, if one goes bad, it affects the others. Life is a juggling act, always changing. Just enjoy the ride and do your best.

Good living is hard work requiring an open mind and a willingness to change. But it's worth the effort.

All my love,

Ri Ri

AKA

Mary W. Watts

P.S. I didn't dream all this stuff up. I read about it, then tested and practiced these skills. You can refer to these tools in *Human Relations*, 4th ed., Cengage Learning, 2011, the textbook I co-authored. Continue to read all you can on these topics, don't stop here. The Internet is full of sound advice.

TABLE OF CONTENTS

PART 1:

DEAL WITH YOURSELF FIRST

YOU CAN ONLY CHANGE YOURSELF

The only person you can change is yourself. This is the most important life lesson.

The good news is we can change our behavior, including our reactions to others.

Of course, there are things we can't alter such as height, eye color, and skin color. Learning to accept and love ourselves is important. Only then can the work to improve begin.

And how do you know what to adjust? By studying your behavior. Figuring out what makes you tick means understanding your emotions, moods, and drives. What punches your button? How does your behavior affect others? What behaviors are not working? How can you approach a similar situation differently?

A code of ethics is important. How are you planning to live your life? Here are some great ones: honesty, fairness, leadership, integrity, compassion, respect, responsibility, loyalty, and law-abiding. Please add to this list.

One error some people make is to believe whatever happens to them is someone else's fault. It may or may not be. Examining the facts and assessing your behavior will clarify the situation. If you contributed to it, take responsibility.

POSITIVE SELF-ESTEEM

Maintaining positive self-esteem is essential. When we feel bad about ourselves, everything breaks down. Staying upbeat by believing in, loving, understanding, and forgiving our imperfections is crucial. Inner voices play a key role in positive self-esteem. It helps control our behavior by evaluating us as we strive toward goals. *Did I make the right choice?* That voice even helps us brainstorm to manage sticky situations. Without it, we can't function in the world or achieve goals. Creating, connecting, and defining ourselves would be impossible.

But sometimes the inner voice goes nuts. We become obsessed about what's bothering us: present stresses, looming anxieties, painful recollections. Setbacks look bigger than they are. These repetitive, anxious thoughts send us spiraling down a rabbit hole, unable to climb out.

I've gone down that path so many times, it isn't even funny. In junior high, I made second chair French horn in the all-city band by practicing hard; knowing every piece inside and out. The next year, I placed much lower, barely making the cut. Admittedly, I didn't practice as much; the poor showing was my fault. Hiding in my room, I cried, blamed myself, and replayed the catastrophe over and over in my mind. Spiraling into deep despair, I thought my life was over.

What can you do to shove the negative voices back in line?

- Vent to a friend but do this sparingly. People get tired of others who gripe and whine all the time.
- Write out your thoughts and feelings.

- Address yourself with your name or "you." Just try it, like a new food. For example, "RiRi, you are blowing this all out of proportion. This is not the end of the world."
- Imagine yourself as a fly on the wall, looking down at the situation. If you were advising a friend from afar, what would your guidance be?
- Focus on the big picture. Things change; this won't last forever.
- Examine what happened and realize it could have been worse.

Maintaining positive self-esteem takes constant work. It's a never-ending battle. At times I felt so bad about myself that I hung a piece of paper on my bathroom mirror about being a competent person and read it daily. When you become overly critical of yourself, stop. Think about your positives. Visualize yourself doing well. Be OK with who you are.

CONTROLLING YOURSELF

Self-regulation is another valuable tool. Many people think this is a free country and you can say or do anything you want. Behaving this way will result in very few friends and most likely no job.

Controlling or redirecting impulses and moods that are disruptive is key. If someone insults you, you may want to yell or shove them. However, being able to stop and think before acting is vital.

Some techniques are counting to ten, taking a walk, talking about it with a trusted friend, sleeping on it, or writing a pros and cons list.

Assessing what happened—and why—is the first step to finding a solution, and you can't do that while in a fit of rage.

While in college, I went with a friend to Italy. We were waiting in a long line to obtain information on transportation to our hotel in Rome. I found myself getting angry and impatient. Duh! It dawned on me that I had a choice—either be upset and go crazy or just chill. Either way, the line was not going to move any faster. Then, too, I probably wouldn't have gotten any help by being mad and annoyed.

PERFECTION AND WINNING

For some reason, our family has a problem with perfectionism. We beat ourselves up because we're not perfect. And winning is everything.

When things don't go our way, we are likely to stomp off in a huff, quit trying, or announce we don't want to play anymore.

My momma, Mary Watson, gave me the best advice ever. *You don't have to be the best but do your best.* Tell yourself this every day. No one, even you, can be perfect.

Look at what you have done as an accomplishment, even if not flawless. Turn mistakes into learning opportunities. Don't let fear of failure stop you from trying something new.

Be sure you understand that, when taking risks, be smart about it. Weigh its' potential positives and negatives. For instance, running across six lanes of traffic on a busy highway at night wearing all black is **not** an intelligent risk. You will most likely end up flat as a pancake.

One of the biggest gambles I ever took worked out well for me. While networking, a woman asked me to collaborate on writing a textbook. I wasn't even a professor and didn't have a full-time job! My biggest writing project had been creating management training for a small consulting company.

After saying "Yes," fear struck. Had I set myself up for failure? In the end, the risk was worth it. Stepping out of my comfort zone resulted in the textbook, *Human Relations* 4th*ed.*, by Dalton, Hoyle, and Watts.

Long-distance bicycle rides were my go-to exercise when your mothers were teenagers. One asked why bother if you never win. There's more than being first. Working on your personal best makes you a champion. Not participating for fear of failure would have deprived me of experiencing the pleasure of long-distance cycling.

When you fail, analyze what happened and how it could have been different. Flunked a test? Did you study as much as you could? Would tutoring help? Do what you need to do and then, forgive yourself and move on. As one of your mothers loves to remind me, *it is what it is.* You can't change the past, so try not to stew about it. (Again, this is hard and takes practice. I routinely remind myself of this.)

When your best isn't good enough and the path is barred, search for a detour. Girlfriend/boyfriend/significant other dumped you? Didn't land the job you wanted? Don't just give up and pout, venting the world is against me. Find another way to get what you need (see the section on wants versus needs). You're likely to find a new world you didn't know existed.

I've hit dead ends many times. Once, a new boss took over and fired me. Thank goodness. My next job was a much better one, leading to my career in human resources.

ASKING FOR HELP

There is absolutely nothing wrong with asking for help. It's not a sign of incompetence, weakness, or inferiority. To me, it's the smart thing to do. First, try to find a solution yourself. If you can't figure it out, consider the best persons to ask. Speak with them privately, explaining the situation. Don't just dump the problem in their laps and walk off. This should be a collaboration. Learn from the experience. You may explain the dilemma and add, "I'd like to pick your brain.... What are your thoughts?"

Ultimately you do not have to follow their recommendations. Rather, use it as a springboard to solve problems by considering new ideas and fresh perspectives.

Never be afraid to reach out to a mental health professional. Counselors have a unique view of the world and are trained to help you sort through your feelings to map the best path forward.

BEING IN CONTROL

We all like to order others around and have things go the way we want. But guess what? You can't control everything and the sooner you learn this, the happier you will be.

Sometimes you need to stand up for yourself; sometimes you need to walk away—possibly run. Try to analyze the situation and make the best choice.

This doesn't mean you should let others totally control you. In all relationships, give and take should exist. I subscribe to the Goldilocks philosophy, *not too much, not too little, but just right.*

If you are in a relationship with no give and take, please re-examine it. Something's not right. If, after working with the other person, a balance is not restored, it may be time to move on.

WANTS VERSUS NEEDS

I want many things and, at times, still do. When your mothers were young, bread machines were all the rage. To me, it was a must-have. But guess what? I haven't used it in years. Keeping it reminds me that what I want is not always

8

going to make me happy. These days, what brings me joy is being around others and having experiences such as traveling and learning new things. I'd rather spend my money that way than on a fancy car, bigger house, or other material possessions.

Think of it this way. What we need in life is safety and belonging. Being healthy, having fun, and feeling content are essential. Everything else is a "want."

Is what you want contributing to your sense of well-being? If not, then maybe you don't need it.

CHANGE

Everything changes but death and taxes. Don't think so? Look in the mirror. Every day you grow older. Change is stressful—good and bad—because it requires adjustments. Moreover, transformation is coming more quickly due to technology, climate change, and globalization.

And the stress it brings can cause anxiety and even depression. Trouble sleeping, irritability, and stomach upsets can be part of the package. Going to a new job you want, while positive, is stressful. You must learn a new routine, and this pushes you out of your comfort zone.

You most likely feel this way every time a new school year starts. A different teacher brings new ways of doing things. In high school, I had one teacher who trashed my written papers. The experience bent me out of shape.

So, when change comes, as it always will, we have two choices 1) fight or 2) adapt. Adapting is the best bet. Consider the positives in what is happening. View the change as an opportunity to learn new things.

And the teacher who dissed my reports? I adapted, learning how to write in a way that appealed to her, a skill that served me well in the world of work.

POSITIVE VERSUS NEGATIVE ATTITUDES

Your glass is either half full or half empty, you have a choice. Those who have a half-full glass grab more out of life. But, again, this takes work. There's an adage, "You get what you expect." So, if you expect things to go well, they probably will.

Listen to your thoughts. Are they always?:

- I can't do this,
- This is too hard, or
- I don't have enough time.

What if you thought?:

- I can try,
- It will be fun to learn something new, or
- I can juggle a few things and fit this into my schedule.

Surround yourself with optimistic people; contribute to upbeat conversations. Humor is a great way to relieve tension and focus on the positive.

Use the flipside technique, looking at the bright side of what happened. For example, you might think, "I had a wreck and totaled my car, but it could have been worse. I didn't get hurt."

Half-full glasses don't last forever. Again, this takes constant work.

DEFENSE MECHANISMS

Learning about defense mechanisms helped me understand myself and others. Employing these methods decreases our internal stress. Many times, these reactions are unconscious. Being aware of our defense mechanisms allows us to find a better way to work through internal stress.

- **Denial**-denying anxiety exists. For instance, a student may deny the need to study and go to the movies instead.
- **Repression**-pushing stressful thoughts worries or emotions out of mind. Many who have had a traumatic event occur, repress the thoughts so they don't have to deal with them, pretending it never happened or—they can't remember it.
- **Rationalization**-explaining away unacceptable thoughts, feelings, and motives. Shoplifting is OK. Everyone does it.

- **Regression**-returning to previous, less mature types of behavior. When sick, we become childish, wanting others to care for us as they did when we were children.
- **Scapegoating**-blaming other persons or groups. The dog ate my homework. My hero is not a crook. Everyone is just out to get him.
- **Projection**-attributing an unacceptable thought or feeling about yourself to others. I've seen this happen before. Someone starts accusing you of a certain behavior, and you realize that's the behavior they're exhibiting.
- **Displacement**-finding safe, less threatening persons or objects and venting frustration on them. I do displace and have watched others displace many times. It goes like this:

The boss yells at the man. He cannot or will not yell back. He goes home and yells at his wife. She cannot or will not yell back. The wife yells at the child, who cannot or will not yell back. The child kicks the dog.

I've had bad things happen at work and have gone home and yelled at your moms. Yikes! Thank goodness I learned to catch myself and apologize. If someone suddenly attacks you, it's probably displacement. Take a chill pill. It's not personal.

- **Sublimation**-directing socially unacceptable impulses through socially acceptable channels. Perhaps someone prone to violence becomes a police officer or, an individual who has no family to love, throws his/her efforts into helping abandoned cats and dogs.
- **Compensation**-attempting to remove feelings of frustration or inadequacy by excelling in other areas. A student may feel she has no friends and to compensate, hurls herself into excelling in school.

- **Cognitive dissonance**-dealing with conflicting beliefs and attitudes by disregarding, discrediting, or avoiding information that pushes against what we believe.

Someone who vapes, for instance, may view it as a safe way to consume nicotine. Steering clear of information about its dangers or claiming those who are delivering that information are not credible, reduces the stress when vaping.

IMPOSTER SYNDROME

Imposter syndrome is fearing being exposed as a fake because we doubt our skills, talents, or accomplishments. This can hold us back. I suffer from this delusion in two areas of my life. One involves membership in an academic honor society. When attending their events, the imposter syndrome strikes, making me feel unworthy of being in the presence of other members. My guess is this stems from not being accepted at the first three colleges I applied for. University of Texas was my alternative. In those days, anyone who had graduated high school could go. But UT wasn't easy. Many didn't make the cut.

The other involves my fiction writing. My mind tells me I'm not as intelligent or competent as others think. Be on alert and work to avoid this trap.

GRIEF

Grief is deep distress caused by loss. The loss can be the death of a person or pet, a job, or a house due to fire. Loss due to change can also cause grief.

You can't fix it; just give it time. Remember, everyone grieves differently. However, grieving losses and reinvesting in the new brings about growth and joy.

The process of grieving goes through several phases. The first is denial. "I can't believe it's happening. I can't face it." Sometimes, when a loved one dies, the survivors are in denial and will not remove the deceased's belongings.

Then comes the anger. "Why me? It's unfair." On to bargaining. "God, if you don't let this happen, I'll do anything you ask."

Depression ensues. Eventually, we accept the situation and move on. Understand that everyone moves through these steps at a different pace. Be patient with yourself and others during times of loss.

BE A SELF-STARTER

Being a self-starter is one of my biggest accomplishments in life. If something new shows up, I learn these skills on my own by reading books, watching videos, or taking short courses. Waiting for the job to train me was not an option.

While attending college, personal computers did not exist. The only computer courses available in graduate school involved writing Fortran programs on punch cards and feeding them to the mainframe.

Soon, personal computers started to appear. Thankfully, I recognized their importance and began training myself, including taking courses.

Same thing on the job. New software, new technology, new regulations—jump on it. Embrace the learning challenge. Focus on being successful and set higher expectations for yourself.

THE ROLES WE PLAY

We play many roles in life. Parent, spouse, friend, volunteer, student, employee, boss, etc. And, many times, several roles at once. Remember that each role has its own acceptable behavior. Your job is to realize the appropriate behavior for that role. Dress and act properly for that part. If you don't, people won't be comfortable dealing with you.

At one point, I was teaching at an adult business school and dressed as a student on the first day of class. Another teacher came to the classroom and spoke about appearance making a difference. After five minutes, I rose, introducing myself as the instructor. The respect and rapport with these students never developed as with other classes because their first impression was that I was at their level.

So, when being an employee, behave like one. At work, don't act like you're out messing with the gang around the swimming pool. Also, dress the part.

SOCIAL MEDIA

I was never forced to deal with social media such as YouTube, TikTok, Snapchat, Instagram, or Facebook. These mediums can be useful. It's a way to stay connected with friends and meet new ones. YouTube can certainly be entertaining, and you can learn lots of new stuff.

It's not perfect, however, and does have a downside. Putting too much personal information online can catch up with you when you are older and applying for a job. Some companies will scan an individual's social media, looking for reasons not to hire. Additionally, dangerous people who are not who they pretend to be, may try to be your friend and lure you into doing something stupid or life-threatening.

Cyberbullies thrive on social media. Bullies have always been with us—putting us down, making fun of us, laughing at us. I remember them from grade school and junior high. At least I could get away from these tormentors after school. Now, they operate online 24-7.

Then, too, quite often people only post the good things happening to them and not the bad. Seeing only their successes can make you feel like a loser. Do they look like supermodels? Have better clothes and cars than you do? Your friends are hanging out with them, and you weren't invited? It hurts.

Don't leave your phone by the bed or, at minimum, turn off the ringer. It's too easy to get sucked in, scrolling late into the night, leaving you tired and out of sorts the next day.

Lastly, it's addictive. Make a point to give yourself some screen-free time.

USING YOUR TIME WELL

The problem with life is time. We never seem to have enough, so using it wisely is a must.

First, figure out how you're spending it. Are you doing the important things first? If not, perhaps procrastination is the culprit. Procrastination is putting off activities intentionally. This may happen because we don't know what to do or fear failure.

Perfection is another problem. We don't do something because it won't be perfect. Sometimes things just need to be done satisfactorily. As your great-grandmother remarked about housekeeping, "I'll give it a lick and a promise." In other words, the house is adequately clean, not sparkling clean. A passably clean house is better than a dirty one.

Developing a plan is the next step. Learn when you are at your peak. I'm a morning person and tend to tackle hard tasks early.

Unfortunately, our smartphones and other technology can be distracting. Messages come in continuously. If we're working or studying, glancing at every message sets us back, diverting our attention and interrupting concentration. Turning off messaging can be a great time saver.

BALANCE AND SELF-CARE

FRIENDS
FAMILY

WORK
SCHOOL

We can have a full life, but, personally, I don't think we can have it all. Bodies wear out. Relationships must be nurtured. We must work to earn a living. Things change constantly. But taking care of our physical and emotional health is the number one priority. It's a juggling act; don't ignore it.

PART 2:

COMMUNICATION SKILLS

COMMUNICATION MATTERS

The inability to communicate causes 80 percent of the problems at work. My advice is to purposely hone these skills and practice them frequently.

COMMUNICATION FLOW

Being aware of the way communication flows is important. Each has its positives and negatives. The ability to choose the best path for the type of communication you plan to send is vital.

One way. No give-and-take exists in this type of communication. For instance, in the airport, announcements are made about flights starting to board. It works well in this situation, giving out information. But, you have no way to ask the voice coming out of the loudspeaker for clarification or assistance.

Two way. The ability to send and respond is present. At the boarding counter, we speak to the agent and receive clarification on our questions.

Upward. People at the bottom of the organization send information to those in higher positions; teacher aides send messages to the principal.

Downward. People at the top send notifications down; the principal sends messages to the teachers, teacher aides, and students.

Horizontal. People on the same level communicate with each other, such as teacher to teacher.

Formal. This means exchanging official information with people at any level of the organization.

Grapevine. This is gossip.

First, examine your message and figure out the best way to send it. For instance, if the teachers are having special training during the workday, it makes sense to put out a formal, top-down announcement. Using two-way communication would mean contacting each person individually—a waste of time.

On the other hand, if a principal has learned that a parent has an issue with a teacher, the principal should not engage in top-down communication with the teacher. Using two way is the wiser solution as it allows both parties to discuss the issue and come to an understanding.

Sometimes we are afraid to pass bad news to others. Why? Because the receiver of the news may take his/her anger out on the one who delivered it (kill the messenger). Whenever you receive unsettling information, do not punish the messenger. If you do, no one will let you know what's going on.

If the message comes through the grapevine, don't believe it wholeheartedly. While it may have some elements of truth, these messages become easily distorted.

Remember playing the game where everyone sits in a circle, and one whispers a message to the person next to them? The message passes through each participant. In the end, communication is generally garbled, not resembling the original one.

COMMUNICATION BARRIERS

Unfortunately, many roadblocks keep us from communicating effectively. If you recognize yourself using one of these barriers, adjust.

Selective listening. Many times, our minds are made up and we only want to listen to messages that affirm our way of thinking. The rest are ignored.

Value judgments. We may not like the lifestyle or values of the person who is communicating with us and react by discounting their message.

Source credibility. How we view the source of the communication has consequences. If a small child comes into the room and reports a fire, most individuals will react differently to her than to a firefighter who shows up in full gear.

Semantic problems. This is particularly troublesome when dealing with other cultures. During college, I visited with my French pen pal, her sister, and their husbands in her home.

The French language has two words for "you"— *tu* and *vous*. *Vous* is formal; *tu* informal. As a Texan, once I meet someone you are my friend, making our relationship informal. My mistake! After using *tu* with everyone, the women confronted me, accusing me of coming on to their husbands! OMG! Despite having studied French for years, I didn't understand how they used the word.

In-group language. Many groups have unique terms they use to communicate internally, particularly in medicine and the military. For instance, the doctor states, "You have a 1/4" diameter defect in the occipital region of your cranium, specifically in the area of the posterior fossa." *Huh?* She's just told you about a hole in the back of your head that is one-fourth inch wide.

When I started working for the Social Security Administration, it took me several months to understand what everyone was saying. DIB, SSI, oh my gosh. Everything was abbreviated, and no one bothered to give me a translation chart!

While at the Equal Employment Opportunity Commission, a clerk answered an investigator's phone. She told the caller that the investigator was in 'intake' and not available to take the call. The individual called the next day, and the clerk became angry. She had told the caller about intake. However, the caller had no way of knowing that 'intake' was a week-long assignment.

Failing to use terminology that people outside your group comprehend can lead to misunderstandings, making the person unfamiliar with your jargon feel intimidated or stupid. They may not ask for clarification. It is your responsibility to communicate clearly to be understood.

Status differences. Speaking truth to power is difficult. For instance, if you are a teacher aide and have some communication with the principal, it can be difficult to truly express your wants and needs.

Time pressure. We get busy—have places to go, things to do, and people to see. When in a hurry, many of us don't take the time to concentrate on communication.

Communication overload. It's easy to be bombarded with communication, anything from phone calls to texts to people stopping by to talk. When overwhelmed, the tendency is to shut down and not pay sufficient attention to what is being conveyed.

LISTENING

Listening is the most important communication skill. Listening actively is an oxymoron (a combination of conflicting words). To *listen*, we think of being quiet, while *active* brings visions of not being quiet.)

How do you actively listen?

First, find a quiet place free of distractions such as your phone. Listen carefully. Don't fake attention. Don't prejudge the speaker, guessing what they are going to say and planning a rebuttal. Pay attention. Ask for clarification. For instance, you might respond, "Let me be sure I understand, you are angry because...." This lets the speaker know you are listening, otherwise, you wouldn't be able to repeat it back. Also, it gives you a chance to clear up any miscommunication.

Try not to use the word "why." As a child, when my mother asked me why I did something, it meant I was in trouble and was going to be punished no matter the explanation.

Instead of saying "Why did you do that?" try "Explain the reasons you decided to do that."

SPEAKING

Use "I" phrases. In other words, I get upset when you..... not "You make me mad when you...

Remember, you are the one upset. For instance, if a friend borrows your basketball without permission they aren't upset, you are. It's your problem, not theirs. If you accuse them, they will most likely tune you out and the problem will not be resolved.

Don't exaggerate (ALWAYS, NEVER). This will shut things down quickly. For instance, if you say, "You always borrow my basketball without asking" and your friend has asked before, then the discussion diverts to arguing about *always*. Instead, try "I got upset yesterday when you borrowed my basketball without asking."

Using examples helps the other person understand what concerns you.

Don't hit below the belt by calling people names or telling them they are stupid. These behaviors shut off communication.

BODY LANGUAGE

Body language is an extremely important part of the communication process. This involves not only body movements and eye contact but also how your voice sounds and the pace of speech. Remember that when you are reading another person's body language, they are reading yours. One formula suggests that 55 percent of our communication is nonverbal, 38 percent vocal, and 7 percent words only.

This is important when you think about the message you want to send. It's so easy to miss a joke sent through text or email because no voice or other physical cues exist. Things can get misinterpreted. Before you deliver a message, consider what form is better. If it's an emotionally charged subject, face-to-face communication is preferable.

The body language interpretations below are for American audiences. Be aware that body language may differ in other cultures. For instance, in the U.S., good eye contact is seen as positive. In some Asian and African cultures, eye contact is viewed as disrespectful; the less eye contact you have, the more respect you are displaying. When visiting or dealing with those from another culture, study their body language and communication style.

Disagreement is displayed by arms crossed on the chest, closed fists, or sitting with a leg over the arm of a chair.

Impatience or boredom is signified by crossed legs or moving of the crossed leg in a kicking motion. Relaxed core muscles, lowered shoulders, and an indirect gaze can also show boredom as well as disinterest.

Confidence is indicated by making a steeple (fingertips touching) with your hands, hands joined together behind the body, feet up on the desk, elevating oneself, or leaning back in a seated position with both hands supporting your head.

Honesty signs include hand over heart, palms uplifted, looking the person in the eye when speaking, a touching gesture, open hands with palms upward, or arms and legs not crossed.

Frustration can be exhibited as short breaths, tsk, tsk sounds, tightly clenched hands, kicking the ground or an imaginary object, as well as wringing hands.

Sometimes a person will articulate one thing, but body language sends another message. For instance, I may text someone "I love your jacket." Try saying this phrase three ways 1) like you mean it with sincerity, 2) dull and mumbling, or 3) in a sarcastic manner, rolling your eyes. While the words are the same, the body language makes the message, revealing your true thoughts.

COMMUNICATING NEEDS AND FEELINGS

Four basic behavior types are used to communicate needs and feelings— aggressive, passive, passive-aggressive, and assertive. In most instances, assertiveness is the preferred behavior.

While employing **aggressive** behavior, you say what you want, think, and feel, but at the expense of others by using "you" statements to assign blame as well as making threats or accusations. Your attitude can be disrespectful; your air of superiority shows. A tense, demanding voice rounds out your demeanor.

Example: While at the movie theater, the people in front of you are talking, and you can't hear the film. An aggressive person will lean over and menacingly yell, "Shut up!"

The idea is to dominate and humiliate others by being self-righteous, controlling, and superior. And yes, your anger is released. And, while that may make you feel great, the others are often defensive, humiliated, or angry. They resent you and may want revenge. The bottom line is that you succeed but at the expense of others.

27

At the other end of the spectrum is **passive behavior**. Passive individuals avoid saying what they want, think, or feel, and spend time apologizing and putting themselves down, all the while hoping someone will guess what they want. The goal is to avoid unpleasant situations and conflict as well as to be liked. Looking people in the eyes is not part of passive body language. They do not take responsibility for their choices and are anxious, hurt, and disappointed when others don't guess what they want.

Example: At the movie theater, the passive person will not speak, but stew, becoming more and more upset.

But how do others react to this behavior? They may feel guilty, superior, frustrated, or angry. Irritation and pity cause them to lose respect because the individual is such a pushover.

Regularly acting this way causes the passive person's anger to build and eventually, the individual blows up.

Another kind of behavior that happens frequently is **passive-aggressive** behavior. When we are uncomfortable with conflict, we express our emotions indirectly rather than being honest or upfront. This sneaky behavior is more difficult to recognize in ourselves and others. Signs are:

- Giving others the silent treatment by disappearing for a time and/or ignoring texts or emails.
- Refusing to discuss issues. For example, we claim everything is fine while our body language and behavior indicate we are upset.
- Snarky comments such as "If you'll try being smarter, I'll try being nicer." Or "If had a hundred dollars for every smart thing you say. I'd be poor."
- Backhanded compliments. While it is a compliment, it is said with the intent to insult. Some examples are:

"You cleaned up. I didn't even recognize you!"

"You look so great in that photo. I can't even see your pimples!"

"That new haircut looks so much better than your old one."

- Weaponized kindness. We do something kind but in a way that gets back at the person we are angry with. For instance, if I am angry a family member forgot my birthday, I might go to great lengths to celebrate theirs and say things such as, "I could never forget such an important day."
- Insulting someone and claiming we are just kidding. "That's an ugly shirt. I'm just kidding."
- Pretending we don't know how to do something to avoid doing it.

Example: In the movie theater, the passive-aggressive person will comment loudly, "People who talk in the theater are so rude." When the person targeted responds, the passive-aggressive will comment, "I didn't mean it."

Passive-aggressive behaviors feel frustrating, confusing, and stressful for the other people involved. They may respond with passive-aggressive behavior. Again, while the passive-aggressive person may feel a sense of control, this pattern is not productive in the long run. Others find us difficult to deal with and may avoid interacting with us.

Assertive behavior is the preferred behavior. Acting assertively allows you to convey what you honestly want, think, and feel in direct and helpful ways as well as make your own choices while using tact and humor. Assertive persons use "I" phrases and active listening while remaining calm and assured, with a firm voice. Your body is relaxed, head erect. You are confident, successful, and in control.

Example: In the movie theater, the assertive person will say, "Excuse me, I'm having trouble hearing the movie, could you please keep your voice down."

When you behave in this fashion, others respect and value you while feeling free to express themselves. They know where you stand. Often you receive what you want if it is reasonable.

While you should normally be assertive, there are times when you should be passive. For instance, if a robber is waving a gun at you, you do not state, "Please Mr. Robber, I don't feel like being robbed today." You passively hand over the money.

Likewise, if a small child runs into the street, you do not speak assertively, "Please, child, I don't want to see you hurt today." Yelling aggressively will get the child's attention.

COMMUNICATION STYLES
<u>Direct Versus Indirect</u>

Communication styles can be different, and it is important to recognize them. Some individuals are DIRECT. They talk about things and convey facts; compete and one-up. For instance, you might observe someone saying, "I have an iPhone 13." The other person responds, "I have an iPhone 14 pro." (I.e.: I have something better than you have). These goal-oriented communicators solve problems and generally, there is a hierarchy in their group.

On the other end are the INDIRECT communicators. Their conversations concern relationships, convey feelings, and work to gain rapport. Avoiding insults and seeking discussion is key. Saving face and a level playing field are important.

Neither style is right or wrong. However, if you are a direct communicator dealing with an indirect one, you may run into issues.

One evening your grandfather and I were cleaning the kitchen. He said, "We need to run the dishwasher." I agreed. The next morning, he asked why I had not turned it on. His statement was so indirect that I did not realize he expected me to start it. To be honest, if he had told me directly "Start the dishwasher" I would have become angry, feeling he was bossing me around.

I, too, am an indirect communicator. As a supervisor, when employees had a work issue to discuss with me, I would consider their points and then suggest they do "x." All my employees except one picked up on this indirect communication as giving them a direct order.

My frustration built because he would not do as asked. Finally, I realized that he didn't catch my indirect cues. If I had said, "Do it this way," he would have responded. He most likely saw me as wishy-washy and indecisive.

However, a direct supervisor who approaches an indirect employee saying do this by 4 p.m., can be seen as cold and uncaring.

Listen to yourself and to those around you to identify styles. Concentrate on the message rather than the way it's delivered. Ask for clarification. You may need to adapt your style to match the person with whom you are interacting.

High Context Versus Low Context

Cultures and groups can operate in low or high-context modes. Low-context groups value the written or spoken word. They are task-oriented, and results-driven, generally adopting a direct linguistic style. In low-context situations, knowledge is more transferable and available to the public.

Baseball, for instance, is low context. The rules are clearly defined and available to anyone. We can maneuver through airports because they are clearly marked. The U.S. tends to be low context, although many smaller groups can be high context.

Countries such as China, Brazil, and France tend to be high context. This means that they are more difficult to penetrate. Long-term relationships are important, and communication is less verbally explicit. Strong boundaries define who is accepted and who is considered an outsider. Many times, decisions and activities focus on face-to-face relationships and often around one person who has authority. Family events, small businesses, regular "pick-up" games, and groups of friends are often high context.

When I first moved to Fayette County, Texas in the early 2000s the Fayette County Fair was high context. For instance, the newspaper announced that carnival rides would be the same price as last year, leaving me clueless as to the cost. The locals knew the price. Also, it said to buy tickets from a fair queen. What? How do you contact them? Again, those who had been in the community for years understood what to do.

Entering a high-context group may be difficult. Additionally, many situations have both high and low context aspects. For example, membership in a nonprofit organization may be open to anyone but may have a high-context core group in charge of the organization.

Assess your circumstances and, if you find yourself in a high-context situation, be patient. You may need to seek input from an established member of the group to learn the unwritten rules and the way the group functions. Lastly, make it a point to assist newcomers in assimilating into high-context cultures in which you operate.

Conversation Rituals

Conversational rituals are things we say that we don't literally mean to make our interactions sociable. For instance, many of us ask, "How are you?" and do not expect or want the other person to tell us the truth—his/her life sucks. This is simply a way to be kind.

Sometimes this backfires if the other person isn't aware of your goal. An example is uttering "I'm sorry," but not really meaning it. We're not taking blame or apologizing, merely trying to convey we care about the other person's situation.

Other rituals include remarking "thanks" at the end of a conversation when there's nothing to thank the other for or using fighting, razzing, teasing or mock-hostile attacks, not expecting the other person to take this behavior seriously.

I have a friend who hung out with a group of guys but finally quit seeing them as often. The teasing and razzing got to him. Be sure not to overdo this.

Regional Differences

Regional differences can cause misinterpretations. Many Northerners, for instance, get directly to the point. No small talk. When I worked with the Red Cross Hurricane Rita relief in East Texas, many Northerners arrived eager to help. But their conversation style appeared rude to the locals. Part of my training ritual was to clue the volunteers in on the regional differences, teaching them to use phrases such as, "Hi, how you doing? What about the weather?" before they got down to business. The feedback was that they were more successful in their mission.

But it works both ways. One Northerner told me he became so frustrated when he went to a fast-food restaurant in Houston because the order takers would want to chat: he just wanted his food.

The bottom line:

To be a competent communicator, you must consistently work to listen and to understand. Only then can you respond in a compassionate, intelligent manner. Communication is the bond that holds relationships of all types together. Without satisfying connections, our life is poorer.

PART 3:

DEALING WITH OTHERS

YOU CAN'T CHANGE OTHER PEOPLE

The most important lesson to remember when dealing with others is YOU CAN'T CHANGE THEM. Accept them as they are. You're not perfect, and neither are they. If they do change, be surprised and grateful.

Treat others with dignity and respect, even if you intensely dislike what they stand for. Everyone deserves this type of treatment because they are human. Don't talk down to someone, using an air of superiority. Talk to them at their level using words appropriate to their understanding. Be real.

This is hard work, practice it daily.

EMPATHY IS YOUR FRIEND

Empathy means you can see a situation from another's point of view. Only then can you attempt to understand their feelings. It doesn't mean you agree with their thoughts, simply that you understand where they're coming from. Until you are in this zone, real discussions cannot begin.

To show empathy, listen actively and without judgment. Ask questions to grasp their viewpoint. If you've had similar thoughts, and are comfortable, share them.

Remember, their feelings are their feelings, whether you agree or not. For instance, perhaps you broke your game controller, and you are going ballistic. I may think it's not a big deal. However, I can confirm your feelings, even while believing they are inappropriate. "I can see you are upset" just means I acknowledge you are upset, not that I think you should be. This goes a long way to opening the channels of communication for future discussion.

KINDNESS

Being friendly, generous, and considerate to others is the key to interacting with those around you. Thinking this way is not enough, you must show it through your behavior. Acting kindly can be as small as being empathetic and accepting. Give compliments. A smile; an unexpected, good deed; a planned surprise; forgiving ourselves and others for mistakes. Helping others without expecting something in return is crucial. BUT it must be sincere.

BUILDING TRUST IS KEY

If people can't trust you, you have a big problem. Saying "trust me" doesn't cut it. You must behave in ways that build it.

You can do this by:

- Doing what you promise.
- Not talking behind people's backs.
- Being consistent.
- Turning mistakes into learning scenarios for yourself and others.
- Believing in individuals—you will get what you expect.
- Learning to declare, "I'm sorry."
- Keeping everyone informed.

Just like everything else, building and keeping trust is a continuous process.

HOW PEOPLE SEE THE WORLD

We are a diverse country—others have different values, thoughts, and feelings than we do. Perceptions develop from our culture and heredity, the time and place where we were born and grew up, and the influence of our peers, shaping our view of the world.

One of my favorite poems is by John Godfrey Saxe:

The Blind Man And The Elephant

It was six men of Indostan, to learning much inclined,
who went to see the elephant (Though all of them were blind),
that each by observation, might satisfy his mind.

The first approached the elephant, and, happening to fall,
against his broad and sturdy side, at once began to bawl:
"God bless me! but the elephant, is nothing but a wall!"

The second feeling of the tusk, cried: "Ho! what have we here,
so very round and smooth and sharp? To me tis mighty clear,
this wonder of an elephant, is very like a spear!"

The third approached the animal, and, happening to take,
the squirming trunk within his hands, "I see," quoth he,
the elephant is very like a snake!"

The fourth reached out his eager hand, and felt about the knee:
"What most this wondrous beast is like, is mighty plain," quoth
he; "Tis clear enough the elephant is very like a tree."

The fifth, who chanced to touch the ear, Said; "E'en the blindest
man can tell what this resembles most; Deny the fact who can,
This marvel of an elephant, is very like a fan!"

The sixth no sooner had begun, about the beast to grope,
than, seizing on the swinging tail, that fell within his scope,
"I see," quothe he, "the elephant is very like a rope!"

And so these men of Indostan, disputed loud and long,
each in his own opinion, exceeding stiff and strong,
Though each was partly in the right, and all were in the wrong!

So, oft in theologic wars, the disputants, I ween,
tread on in utter ignorance, of what each other mean,
and prate about the elephant, not one of them has seen!

Remember: when we see or hear something, it's only one piece of
the puzzle. Reserve judgment until you've filled in as many pieces as
possible.

PERCEPTION IS EVERYTHING

That brings me to the idea that perception is everything. Whether what someone perceives is true or not, it is their reality.

For instance, as a child, my brother would try to scare me to get a rise out of me. I learned to not react to what he was doing. Soon he got bored and left me alone. This ability came in handy when investigating employment discrimination. Showing no emotion when someone told me something horrific allowed me to collect more information than if I had reacted with body language.

While good in one sense, it was bad in another. Saying "Good morning," to a co-worker with no emotion, left the incorrect perception that I wasn't happy to see them. I finally learned to put some feeling into it and smile, making my voice *sound* glad to see them.

I could listen to your mothers tell me something, not looking at them, multi-tasking, cleaning the kitchen. By not giving listening cues, they perceived I was not paying attention, which was not the case. Be sure you are sending the message you want to send through your statements and actions.

Also, don't blow off someone's perception. If it is incorrect, move to clarify it immediately.

DIMENSIONS OF DIVERSITY

You are fortunate to have grown up in an area of the country that is ethnically diverse. Please expand your understanding of diversity to include more than race, ethnicity, sex, and sexual orientation. Upbringing, age, physical abilities, education, religious beliefs, personal experiences, parental status, income, occupation, marital status, geographic location, and military experience add to the diversity of our nation. And the better you are at dealing with people who are different from you, the better off you will be.

All humans stereotype and have biases and prejudices. These behaviors are coded deep inside our DNA, most likely from the cave people days when someone from the outside might be dangerous, by attacking you or bringing disease.

Stereotyping, believing something fits into a general pattern, frames the way humans maneuver through life. We learn, for instance, that a moving car can hurt us if we walk in front of it. When seeing types of vehicles (trucks, smaller or larger cars) we transfer that knowledge to the new situation. Failing to do so would force us to learn this lesson for every vehicle on the road.

While stereotyping makes our lives easier in some respects, it can turn out badly when dealing with human beings as they are frequently involved in biases and prejudices.

A bias is a preference either for or against an individual or group. It keeps us from being impartial. Prejudice, on the other hand, involves making decisions about other people or groups without sufficient knowledge.

When working for the Equal Employment Opportunity Commission investigating employment discrimination, I had a case involving a Nigerian male. He was difficult to work with and insulted me as a female. Before this interaction, I had no experience with Nigerians. My next case involving a Nigerian left me upset. I complained to a friend.

He said, "Nigerian...Nigerian? I love Nigerians. They are warm, wonderful people." It dawned on me that I had been stereotyping, taking a characteristic of one individual and assigning that characteristic to everyone in their group! And I knew better! My job was to go after others who did the same thing.

The scary thing is that we all have definite, entrenched stereotypes by the age of five. We absorb them as if by magic, from our environment. At this age, we haven't had the ability or experiences to form our own beliefs.

I gave one of your mothers a toy doctor kit for her fourth birthday. She looked at me and said, "I can't have this." When I asked why, she said, "Girls can't be doctors." I was horrified. No one had told her that, but I soon realized that she had never been to a female doctor before. She just sucked this viewpoint out of her environment.

At the age of two, one of you had an accident at church and no clean underwear. The teacher put you in a pink diaper, and you went ballistic! Why? Boys don't wear pink.

The book *Bridging Cultural Conflicts* by Michelle LeBaron shares the story of Chinese Scholar Professor Zheng Wang:

"I was born in a divided society—in a small town. There were two groups of people—local indigenous people, most of them "Bai" people, a minority ethnic group in China, and outsiders. My parents, their colleagues and families were all "Han Chinese," a majority group in China. Outsiders were sent to the small town by the government to build a hydro-power station. As a child, I knew I was different from the local people. They are poor and dirty, they did not go to school and were ignorant. I knew I should not play with the local children. I do not remember that we had disputes with the local people, just not much communication."

Every human on this planet has biases and prejudices. We develop them naturally and can't help it. But we can do something about it! Exploring and understanding our biases and prejudices and how they impact others is crucial. Then, we must accept responsibility for the way we behave—and change.

Furthermore, we must repeatedly check ourselves to be sure we're not falling into this trap. It's a lifelong thing, like working on your self-esteem. I should know. Having taught people not to stereotype for years, I went into the new cell phone store that opened near my house. A man who appeared to be in his seventies approached me. (I was in my sixties when this happened.) My brain went into overdrive. a voice inside me said, *"I hope he doesn't try to help me; he seems too old to answer my questions about Galaxy smartphones."* Thank goodness I caught myself and accepted his help. (Because you're old doesn't mean you don't understand computers and cell phones.) He quickly turned me over to a young person, explaining he was a regional executive just there for the opening.

Several days later, I went back to the store with technical questions. The people brought in for opening day were gone and the young person who helped me didn't know any more about the Galaxy than I did. Go figure.

One of the problems we have is that, if we have not learned to recognize and check our own biases and prejudices, we CAN discriminate when in a position of power,.

Anyone can do this regardless of race, religion, sex, national origin, age, or disability. The favored group can discriminate against the non-favored group.

VALUES ARE AT THE HEART OF EVERY DECISION WE MAKE

Values underscore every decision we make. Values cause sane people to come up with different conclusions about the same problem. When we are in a group of diverse people, decision-making becomes difficult. However, because all sides of the issue are explored, the decision tends to be better. In the end, sometimes we need to agree to disagree.

To illustrate this concept, I did the following exercise during company training on diversity thousands of times. I told the participants beforehand that there were no right or wrong answers. All the characters were flawed.

THE FLOOD

Once upon a time there was a man named Joe who had a good friend named Susan. Susan lived in the next kingdom. One day a terrible flood hit Susan's kingdom. Her house filled with water, and she lost all her worldly possessions. Susan called Joe to tell him of the damage the flood had caused and how she had nowhere to sleep and nothing to eat.

Joe was so upset that he approached his boss and asked if he could have a few items to give to Susan, who was suffering greatly. The boss was extremely wealthy and owned a chain of stores. He had millions of dollars in the bank and warehouses full of household goods. The boss flatly refused to help, but said Joe was free to buy what his friend needed. Distressed, Joe went to talk to his mother, who had some savings set aside. His mother listened and then said, "It's your problem; I don't want to get involved."

So Joe, who had no money, decided he would take the things from the boss's warehouse. He backed his pickup truck up to the warehouse and filled the truck with everything Susan needed. On his way to deliver the supplies he came to a drawbridge. The drawbridge operator refused to let Joe through unless he paid a fare. Joe then had to give the operator some of the goods for Susan, as he had no money.

At last, he arrived at what remained of Susan's home. She was so grateful for the supplies; she began to cry. Everything was fine until Joe told her how he got the items. Enraged, Susan began yelling at him, saying she was embarrassed to know a thief and did not want to have anything to do with the items Joe had given her. Angry and humiliated, Joe left.

When Joe again saw the drawbridge operator, he explained how cruelly Susan had treated him. The drawbridge operator was sympathetic and said that he would punish her by not allowing her to escape across the drawbridge. Joe was happy to hear that Susan would suffer for her cruelness.

Exercise: Please rank the characters in order from one to five. One will be the character you think is the most offensive and five being the least offensive. There is no correct answer to this exercise. In a group discussion, identify why you made the choices you did and how your decisions trace back to your value system.

In thousands of attempts, a group **never** agreed on the ranking. Some, for instance, would rate Joe as the worst because he stole; others, the best because he was the only one trying to help. Many had issues with Mom for not assisting her son while the remainder felt she was within her rights. The boss was rich, it was his obligation to share the wealth. Another faction felt it was his money, and he could do with it what he wanted. Why?

Values.

Those, particularly the police officers, valued law and order over helping someone. The participants who were upset that Mom had not helped, grew up in a household where mothers were the glue of the family and were expected to do everything possible for their children. Others were raised in homes where, once you turned eighteen, Mom said "goodbye" and "don't let the door hit you on the behind as you leave."

CULTURAL WORLD VIEWS

MOTHER EARTH

ARE WE ON THE SAME Planet?

Different cultures around the world have varying viewpoints. When dealing with others, it's important to be able to recognize these patterns to better understand where the individual is coming from. Again, these ways of seeing things are neither right nor wrong.

Individualism versus Collectivism

An individualistic culture is one in which the individual is held as more important than the whole. The collective culture values the group above the individual.

Collective cultures such as Japan put greater emphasis on common goals than on individual pursuits; the rights of families and communities come before those of the individual. They have a saying that "The nail that sticks out gets hammered down." Americans tend to thrive on individualism, believing that every person is unique and self-reliant. "The squeaky wheel gets the grease."

Self-determination versus Fate

Self-determination is the belief that we control our future through our actions. Americans believe in self-determination. *Pull yourself up by the bootstraps! You can be anything you want to be!*

Other cultures, however, believe in fate, that our path is set by the Gods, an invisible hand, or the universe—we cannot change it. *Everything happens for a reason!*

Equality versus Hierarchy

In societies such as the U.S. and Australia, equality means that anyone can become successful regardless of where they began in life. The U.S. is full of rags-to-riches stories. Individuals are seen as equals; power and status differences are minimized.

However, for hierarchical cultures such as India and China, social ranking is fixed at birth and unlikely to change. Members show respect and admiration for those in power and authority.

Doing versus Being

Getting things done is the *doing* mindset. Setting goals and working towards them is key. Americans tend to inhabit this mindset.

In the *being* mode, however, the mind focuses fully on moment-by-moment experiences, being present and aware of what is going on around us.

Linear Time versus Fluid Time

Linear-time cultures such as the U.S., see time as a resource to be thoroughly planned and managed. Planning for delays to stay on schedule is our responsibility. Promptness and being on time are important.

Flexible-time cultures such as India, Saudi Arabia, Mexico, and most African countries tend to view time as uncontrollable. Sticking to a strict schedule is not expected.

WORK STYLE DIFFERENCES

Besides value differences, workstyle differences are common. Allow individuals to work in the way they are comfortable. Some follow a monochronic style, following plans closely and doing one thing at a time. Polychronic workers, on the other hand, do many things at once, change plans, and tolerate interruptions.

UNCERTAINTY

Because we see things differently, dealing with others takes work. We should expect uncertainty. What we see and think may not be another person's reality. We must accept this and go with the flow, being flexible. You may never completely understand a situation; just live with it.

TOOLS FOR DEALING WITH PERCEIVED BIASES AND PREJUDICES

Sometimes people will say something that offends us. Was it on purpose or was it unintentional? Before flipping out, try to evaluate the situation. Think about what was said. Could it have more than one meaning? Examine the context of the statement. Context refers to the interrelated situation in which an event occurs, i.e., the big picture.

For instance, early in my career, I worked with a man who irritated me by calling me "honey," "darling," and "sweetheart". I felt he was demeaning me as a woman. How could a "honey" be a strong competent person? But, instead of attacking him, I thought about it, putting it in context. He never said or did anything else that indicated he disliked or disrespected women. In fact, he connected me with one of his female friends who later became my writing partner for the textbook! He was born and raised in Texas and using these terms is common. I concluded it was only his manner of speech and not an indication of how he viewed my skills and abilities.

If someone has said something to offend you, try the following techniques to resolve the issue:

- Be clear about your goals for challenging the individual.
- Try to assume goodwill (the other person did not realize what he or she said was offensive).
- Talk to the person privately.

- Be honest and direct when explaining how the comments made you feel.
- Use "I" phrases.
- Give examples of the comments and behaviors that offended you.

If you have been told you're offensive, do the following:

- Listen intensely and reserve judgment.
- Ask questions to clarify the other person's concerns.
- Apologize if you had no intention of offending that individual.
- Do not use the phrase or word that was offensive in the future out of respect for the individual even if you don't understand why it upset him/her.

For instance, I began practicing my Spanish on my older Hispanic, male friend. When we would pass in the hall I would say, "Hola Senior Cruz." After a while, he became angry and told me to stop that.

My first reaction was to be offended. After all, I'm trying to learn his language. Why was this offensive? But, I apologized and never said it again out of respect for him.

OTHER STUFF YOU NEED TO KNOW IN NO SPECIAL ORDER

RiRi's GRABBAG
OF IMPORTANT
STUFF!

POWER

Power is our ability to influence others to do what we want them to do even if we aren't the formal leader. Power can be positive when used in positive ways. You must have power before you can influence. Understanding power is crucial to success.

Types Of Power

Legitimate.	You are the boss or hold a high position.
Reward.	You use rewards to get someone to act.
Coercive.	You use force or threats to get what you want.
Expert.	You have special skills, knowledge, or expertise.
Referent.	You are respected and admired for your past achievements.
Derivative.	You are linked to a powerful person.
Passive.	You pretend to be helpless to get assistance with a task or get out of it altogether.

Be mindful of how you use the power you have. If you are in a position of leadership, you need to determine how each individual responds to coercive and reward power before deciding whether or how much of it to use.

Passive power won't get you far and neither will derivative power. Stay away from these if possible.

POLITICS

I used to think that being good at what I did was the only thing necessary for success. Wish it were true, but, the reality is, to be successful we must be technically proficient and play group politics.

Group politics consists of informal efforts by members to position themselves and their teams to get their interests and priorities met. These behaviors occur in work groups, volunteer groups, school clubs, or groups of friends and include unethical as well as ethical actions.

Don't try to cut others down; play fairly. Go for a win-win situation, where each person is better off. Everyone has an opinion, and, to move forward, we must work to change them.

The method of changing opinions I find effective is to drop little seeds pointing to your way of thinking. This gives the other individual a chance to consider what you have said.

Remember, you can't change others, but you can gradually reveal your viewpoint on the issue. Then, too, learning others' opinions is crucial. You can't work for a win-win situation if you don't know what they want.

For instance, you may have an informal group that you game with over the Internet. Want to change the game you are playing? Times? Let others into the group? These terms must be negotiated and benefit everyone.

Once, as a new human resource manager, I had a mess on my hands. Our hiring process was a disaster. We had different groups in the same company working against each other to hire the same person! Then, too, when people came on board, they could not get the equipment they needed to start work in a timely fashion.

Because I had no supervisorial authority, dictating the fix was impossible. So, I called together the employees involved in this process, and presented the issue to them, soliciting suggestions and making recommendations. After several sessions, I had everyone on board, and we rolled out a fabulous system that was a win-win for all.

PAYBACK

Everyone expects to be paid back. Ever heard the saying, "I'll scratch your back if you scratch mine." Giving and taking is a way of life. If you give a friend a ride to and from soccer practice or a restaurant and they never give back by treating you to a dessert, paying for gas, or driving, it brings up bad feelings. Be sure to find a way to pay back kindness.

This happens all the time at work. Once I went with my boss to visit a very successful new car salesman. He shuffled through a large batch of business cards. Eventually, he pulled one out and asked us to visit with this individual. The link resulted in new business. By doing favors for others, he obtained scads of new customers. Who would you buy a car from—a total stranger or someone who helped you earn money to make the car payment?

SUCCESS BREEDS CONTEMPT

Sometimes, when you are successful, others become jealous and may try to undermine you. When you realize this is happening, take the offensive. Kill them with kindness, don't become angry or vengeful or avoid them. For instance, if you got picked for the varsity soccer team and your friend didn't, perhaps he's being rude to you because he's jealous. Rather than avoiding him, be friendly. Speak kindly. "Wish you could have been on the team with me." It's hard for someone to continue to be mean to you when you are kind.

COMPLIMENTS

Assume the compliment is sincere. If someone remarks they like your shirt, respond with thank you rather than "I like your shirt, too." Don't diminish the praise by saying something like, "This is just an old rag I found in the bottom of the closet." If it makes you feel good, let the other person know.

Lastly, give yourself compliments if no one else does.

TRIANGLES

Don't get drawn into other people's problems. A "triangle" occurs when one person brings you into a problem that he or she is having with a third person. Stay out of it. For instance, Jean is mad at her mother and asks you to talk to her mother about the issues between the two of them. You do not have a dog in this hunt. You can empathize with Jean, but Jean needs to handle this herself.

Be ready to support others by being a sounding board. Listen and, if asked, make suggestions. But don't expect them to do exactly as you suggest and don't own their problems. You did not cause the problem, and it is not your responsibility to fix it.

LACK OF INFORMATION

When people lack information, they put the worst possible thoughts in to fill the void. For instance, you're late and have stayed out past your curfew. Your parents will think you have died in a car wreck rather than that you got busy chatting with a friend and lost track of the time.

Moral: Keep others informed so they don't dream up stuff.

THINKING YOU KNOW IT ALL

You are all sharp as whips and that might lead you to fall into the trap of thinking you know it all. And maybe you do. One thing I've learned in life is that I don't understand everything. After graduating from college, despair overcame me; I hadn't learned everything possible about my major.

But if you act like you know everything all the time, you'll fall into a pit of trouble. If you think you are right, don't immediately correct someone. Remember, you could be wrong. Try some qualifiers such as "I think" or "perhaps." Sometimes their mistakes aren't worth correcting. Think about that before you judge. If your friend is telling a story and saying you went to the 7 p.m. movie when it was 8 p.m., does it matter?

HANDLING CONFLICT

Conflict is everywhere! Personality clashes, disagreements about politics, work, religion, or even what color to paint the living room. Conflict is routine in the family and the workplace. So, rather than avoiding it, learn to deal with it. Because, if handled correctly, it can be a positive force, especially if it centers around ideas and issues.

The first thing you need to do when you are either in a conflict with another person or are working with individuals or groups in conflict is to listen actively. Work to uncover needs, don't assume you are aware of them. Remember, what they *want* may not be what they *need*.

Suppose you're into goth and want to paint your room black and decorate it with decals. Your parents object. Rather than just throwing a fit, talk to them calmly to find out why they object. You might be surprised. Once you realize how hard it is to paint over black walls (you need to paint a primer and then possibly two coats of paint) you may begin to see their point. Only then can you and your parents work towards an agreement.

One time, when I was a human resource manager, an employee we had fired asked for his personnel file (his want). It was our policy not to give them to anyone. We could have come to blows about the issue, but I thought to ask the reason he wanted it. He responded that, if he were aware of what the company said, he would be better able to rebut that information with a potential employer.

Since our policy was not to release information in the file to future employers, his need was met. We only confirmed that he had worked for us and the dates. The conflict was over. Had we not been communicating well; the situation could have ended badly.

One tactic is to ask questions. *For what reason? What if?* My favorite one is "If I could wave a magic wand, what would you want to happen?"

Offer alternative solutions. *A possibility is.... What do you think about...?* Gathering these options is a great starting place for a solution. But be warned, this takes time.

Reframing is a great tool. When doing this you help the other person view the situation from a different perspective. Moving to a new school could be viewed as an opportunity to learn new things and meet new people rather than simply losing everything you are comfortable with.

Sharing experiences can be helpful because it lets the other person understand they are not the only one going through this type of situation.

Discuss both the emotional and financial costs. You've heard the expression, "Be careful what you wish for because you actually might get it." Unfortunately, in the heat of conflict, we frequently fail to think about what we want. You can get to the heart of the matter through a technique called reality testing. By asking questions, you can help the other person focus on his/her needs.

For instance, Hal may be angry with a coworker and complain to his supervisor, insisting he refuses to work with him/her. An excellent reality testing question would be *Are you prepared to be transferred or terminated to resolve the problem?*

You want to sue? Are you aware of how much that would cost? Are you willing to pay the other side's court costs if you lose?

Focus on the future. Solving conflict works to put the past behind us so we can look to the future. The resolution must be a win-win, satisfying the interests of both parties. While no one may have gotten everything they wanted, they are satisfied and can live with the agreement.

Finally, be sure that the solution allows everyone to save face. Many times, others do not want to admit they were wrong or have backed down. You can help the other party save face by granting minor concessions or simply stating your feelings or wishes without making a judgment about the other person. Bragging about your victory is a no-no.

My recommendation is that you learn as much as possible about negotiating and mediating. These enhanced skills have served me well.

BEWARE OF THE TRICKSTERS

There are tons of tricksters in the world who want you to believe certain things. They deliberately spread false information, trying to influence you or hide the truth. They not only do this by the written word, but now they are doing it with Artificial Intelligence. These days they can change or mislabel a picture or video to sway your way of thinking. As I write, the disinformation folks are taking videos of famous persons and altering them to make the people say things they did not say. For instance, a picture of a castle can be placed deep in the ocean as proof of finding archeological ruins. The hustlers may alter a video of rockets pounding an airport runway, claiming it is new, even though the film is over ten years old.

How do we protect ourselves?

A useful way to start is by learning to think critically so you have a better understanding of the issues and decide whether you should believe them. We must gather all the pieces of the puzzle and then come to an informed conclusion.

Some tools are:

Distinguish fact from opinion. Is what you are hearing a fact, a thing that is known to be true, to exist, or to have occurred? Or is it an opinion, a view about a particular issue and is not necessarily true? Many times, the tricksters present opinions as facts. Digging out the truth requires spending time researching their statements.

Remember, dealing with facts can be tricky. A student may claim that Joe shoved him. While this may be true, the statement may be taken out of context. After looking at the whole situation, you may find that the student called Joe names, bullied him, and blocked him from leaving the classroom. Now, the shoving seems warranted where, without the context, it sounds bad.

We can't dismiss opinion. People act on opinions even if not backed up by facts. For instance, we may buy name-brand canned vegetables, believing that they are better than the store brand. This may or may not be true.

Understand the differences between primary and secondary sources. What sources are being used to make the case? A primary source is original material. Examples of primary sources include court records, letters, and government documents. Original research and position papers of organizations are also considered primary sources.

While an eyewitness account is a primary source, a person's report may be colored by their previous experience or their stake in the situation. For instance, the eyewitness description of a traffic accident might be different if told by the driver accused of ignoring a red light than by a person standing nearby who witnessed the accident.

A secondary source consists of information collected from primary sources and then interpreted by the collector. When analyzing secondary sources, remember that the individual is giving their interpretation. You may want to consult several secondary sources. When looking at the interpretation, ask:

- What types of primary sources did the author use?
- Can you be sure the sources are accurate?
- Is it possible that the author's information is skewed by his or her personal views?

Evaluate information sources. Everyone's got a point of view, even if they try to present it objectively. When looking at the source of the information, try to put yourself in their head and figure out what their point of view is.

Ask yourself these questions:

- Who is the source of this information?
- What is his or her point of view?
- When was this written? The writer's opinion might have changed over time.

For instance, a scientist may produce a study showing that Chocolate XXO Bars are a healthy food choice and should be eaten three times a day. After critically evaluating the scientist, you may find he/she was paid by the Chocolate XXO Bar company to conduct the study.

Recognize deceptive arguments. If you're not careful, you can be swayed by others using these tactics:

- Bandwagon—the idea that "everybody" does this or believes this. Commonly held beliefs are not necessarily correct ones. Just because everyone grabs a handful of grapes to eat while shopping in the grocery store doesn't mean it's right.
- Scare tactics—the threat that something terrible will happen if you don't do or don't believe this. If we don't wear a certain type of tennis shoes, we won't be popular or if we don't eat at a certain fast-food establishment we are losers. Unfortunately, in our political climate, scare tactics are alive and well.
- Personal attack—criticizing an opponent personally rather than debating his or her ideas rationally. "You are stupid, look like a dork, and have a funky odor" instead of, "I think your idea of a club project is something we won't be able to finish before the end of school."
- Testimonial—quoting or paraphrasing an authority or celebrity to support one's viewpoint. Companies do this often. Many times, the chosen celebrities have no expertise in the area.

- <u>Straw person</u>—exaggerating or distorting an opponent's ideas to make one's own seem stronger. For instance, a principal wants to change some things at the school. The straw person argument will misrepresent what the principal wants to do by suggesting she wants to ban everything fun at school.
- <u>Slanting</u>—persuading through inflammatory and exaggerated language instead of reason. A taxpayer rants about new textbooks at school, saying the books are a waste of taxpayer money, teach outrageous ideas, and aren't needed. The old ones are just fine.
- <u>Ethnocentrism and stereotypes</u>—framing arguments using stereotypes and ethnocentrism, This thought process holds that our nationality, religion, or cultural traditions as superior to others. The idea that illegal immigrants need to be deported because they take jobs unemployed citizens could do, falls into this category. Recognizing this tactic can better help you evaluate the statement.

DON'T FORGET

We all have subconscious biases and can make mistakes. As humans, we tend to groupthink, a certain amount of our belief system is based on what others say instead of what we have personally witnessed. Lastly, critical thinking skills are one of those things you need to work on, especially with Artificial Intelligence and the changes we are facing.

I have the following hanging on my office wall. My mother gave it to me. I want to share it with you:

Desiderata

Go placidly amid the noise and the haste, and remember what peace there may be in silence. As far as possible, without surrender, be on good terms with all persons.

Speak your truth quietly and clearly; and listen to others, even to the dull and the ignorant; they too have their story.

Avoid loud and aggressive persons; they are vexatious to the spirit. If you compare yourself with others, you may become vain or bitter, for always there will be greater and lesser persons than yourself.

Enjoy your achievements as well as your plans. Keep interested in your own career, however humble; it is a real possession in the changing fortunes of time.

Exercise caution in your business affairs, for the world is full of trickery. But let this not blind you to what virtue there is; many persons strive for high ideals, and everywhere life is full of heroism.

Be yourself. Especially do not feign affection. Neither be cynical about love; for in the face of all aridity and disenchantment, it is as perennial as the grass.

Take kindly the counsel of the years, gracefully surrendering the things of youth.

Nurture strength of spirit to shield you in sudden misfortune. But do not distress yourself with dark imaginings. Many fears are born of fatigue and loneliness.

Beyond a wholesome discipline, be gentle with yourself. You are a child of the universe no less than the trees and the stars; you have a right to be here.

And whether or not it is clear to you, no doubt the universe is unfolding as it should. Therefore be at peace with God, whatever you conceive Him to be. And whatever your labors and aspirations, in the noisy confusion of life, keep peace in your soul. With all its sham, drudgery and broken dreams, it is still a beautiful world. Be cheerful. Strive to be happy.

ADVICE FROM MY FRIENDS

WHAT THEY WOULD TELL THEIR
16-YEAR-OLD SELVES

FROM MY FRIENSS
TO You!

Fawn
Getting married is not the most important thing in life. God comes first then go to college and get a couple of degrees. Maybe even become a veterinarian. That way you can support yourself through life. True love will eventually come your way.

Gary
I don't fit the normal cut, but I don't mind telling you my advice to myself at 16. Actually, it happened at 13. I had a fight with my father over a guitar I bought with my own money. He said he wouldn't have it in his house. After a lot of fighting, he offered me a deal. I could get rid of it or move down into the unfinished basement and could keep the guitar there and never get another penny from him ever again. To his surprise, I chose the guitar. I bought my clothes, food (except for Sunday dinners with the family), school expenses, etc. This caused me to investigate college

opportunities, so I chose the military academies. My advice to myself at 16 was to stay the course, sign up for everything I could and stay out of trouble. In everything I did I strived to not only succeed but excel. There will always come a time when you can count on not anyone but **yourself.**

Marie
Become self-aware of my needs earlier; learn to say no.

Michelle
Stop taking life so seriously. Life is meant to be lived and you are missing out is the number 1 thing I would tell my 16-year-old self.

#2. Find your passion, what you are good at and what excites you. This is what I would look at when you are trying to decide what you want to do with your life. You are going to have to work the vast percentage of your life, you might as well do something that you love.

#3. Don't worry about what other people think you are doing, what they think you should do, or how you should act- you do you, and as long as you are not hurting someone (including you), or are not going to end up in jail then don't worry about it.

You have to lead your life based on your values and beliefs. You can't lead anyone else's life for them nor they for you!

#4 Be the friend you would like someone to be for you. Lifelong friends are rare but can happen if you find real people who will be there through thick and thin times. But both parties have to be willing to be there and actually care about the other. You don't have to have lots of those people in your life, but you have to find one or two that you can keep around, that know you and still love you! the good and the bad. They need to be able to tell you when you are messing up, and you tell them the same. Be willing to tick them off being honest and be willing to hear the hard stuff back.

I think those are the top four.

Linda
Follow your heart without fear.

Catherine
1. It's more important to be open to learning than to get things right on the first try.
2. Asking for help is not weak.
3. Putting yourself first is not always selfish. Sometimes it is self-compassion.
4. Don't be in such a big hurry to accomplish every dream. The journey is where the magic happens.

Gabi
That it's okay to make mistakes, so long as you admit them as soon as you realize. That gives you time to fix them, or at least to make sure they don't get any worse.

Elaine
Just a few things off the top of my head.
1. Be yourself. Don't try to be someone you are not.
2. Stay away from "drama." It is not worth your time or energy. Just walk away.
3. Have a good work ethic. This will help you in the long run.
4. As the song goes, "Make new friends, but keep the old."
5. Spend time with your family. Keep memories of them alive in your mind and heart.
6. Don't carry grudges. It is a waste of time and energy.
7. Give back to others, your community, and the environment.
8. Be thankful for your blessings and find joy in little things.

9. Learn how to manage your money. Many people never learn how to do this!
10. Put down the damn phone and look up. It is more important to make a human connection and appreciate what is around you.
11. Be independent and take care of things yourself. You need to learn how to do laundry, cook, clean, change a tire, start a fire safely, etc.

Katy

Self Confidence is KEY to happiness. Learn it and exhibit it to others. Go to College – or away from home. Learning self-sufficiency. It's key to being self-confident. You can do or be anyone in your later life if you have this key.

Greg

Two maxims have been meaningful to me throughout the decades:

1. A non-denominational version of the Serenity Prayer:

May I have the courage to change the things I can change,
The serenity to accept the things I cannot change,
And the wisdom to know the difference.

2. The quote from Hillel the Elder:

"If I am not for myself, who will be for me?
But if I am only for myself, what am I?
And if not now, when?"

THE END

About the Author

MARIE W. Watts is a former employment discrimination investigator and human resource consultant with over thirty years of experience. She has trained thousands of employees to recognize one's own biases and prejudices and avoid discriminating against others in the workplace, and she has coauthored a textbook about it: *Human Relations, 4th ed.*

Additionally, her work has been published in the *Texas Bar Journal* and the *Houston Business Journal,* as well as featured on *Issues Today,* syndicated to 119 radio stations, NBC San Antonio, Texas, and TAMU-TV in College Station, Texas.

In pursuit of justice in the workplace, Marie has been from jails to corporate boardrooms seeing the good, the bad, and the ugly of humans at work. She brought her experiences to life in the award-winning fiction trilogy, Warriors For Equal Rights.

She and her husband live on a ranch in central Texas. In her spare time, she supports a historic house and hangs out with her grandsons.

Follow Marie and her stories about life at
www.mariewatts.com.

www.ingramcontent.com/pod-product-compliance
Lightning Source LLC
Chambersburg PA
CBHW060420050426
42449CB00009B/2052